EXPLORING MAUI

WITH

KIDS

A Jr. Travelers Series Memory Book

Publication and Copyright 2013
Travelers Series Publishing, LLC
11858 Bernardo Plaza Ct.
Suite 230
San Diego, CA 92128
Printed in the United States

JR. TRAVELERS SERIES

Dear Jr. Traveler,

We hope you're excited about a great vacation! Your memory book is filled with many challenges, including pictures, trivia, scavenger hunts and collections. It can be fun to work with your family or friends to complete the challenges together. Do your best, but remember that the most important part of any activity is to collect the sights, smells, and sounds of your family adventure.

Be sure to visit us online at TravelersSeries.com to learn about other Jr. Travelers Series products and destinations. Wherever your family adventure takes you, we're glad you're taking us along for the ride. Happy traveling!

Sincerely,

The Bowers and Medley families

Co-Founders, Travelers Series Publishing

 DO IT!

Sometimes you will want to collect things that won't fit on the pages of your memory book. Other times, you will visit places that are not in the book. Before you leave on your trip you need to create a "Souvenir Saver" to store mementos like pictures, tickets, receipts, menus and more. You can also attach them to the blank pages at the back of this book.

1. Find a manilla envelope with a string or metal clasp.

2. Decorate the envelope with drawings or other artwork.

3. Write "Souvenir Saver" on the envelope.

4. Use your Souvenir Saver to collect mementos from your trip!

Maui

PASSPORT TO MAUI, HAWAII
USA

Tape your favorite
Hawaii picture here.

Tip: Be sure to take your pictures sideways, because your Jr. Travelers Memory book is designed to fit pictures horizontally.

CHALLENGES

Surfboard Count CHALLENGE!

Hawaii is famous for its large waves and scores of surfers. With so many great beaches to catch a wave, Hawaiians love to shoot the curl. You will see locals and tourists alike sharing their love of surfing. Count how many surfboards you see during your trip - in the water, on the beach and on top of cars. Use the box to the right to tally up your sightings and write the total on the line below the box!

Total: _____

Tiki Statue CHALLENGE!

The word "tiki" refers to stone and wood carvings made in a human shape. These statues are a part of Polynesian Mythology and can be found throughout the Hawaiian islands. Today, you can find just about anything made with a tiki - placemats, cups, pens, key chains, t-shirts, candy and more! Count how many different tikis you find, write down the most interesting tiki, and take a picture and store it in the Souvenir Saver!

Total: _____

The most interesting tiki I saw was: _____

Aloha State Flower CHALLENGE!

Hawaii is full of exotic flowers and they come in a seemingly never-ending array of bright and beautiful colors! Enjoying the floral diversity of Hawaii is another way to truly appreciate the magic of the islands. As you explore this tropical state try to find two different types of flowers for each of the colors listed to the right. Check the box when you find each of the two flowers and do your best to label the type of flower you found by asking those around you or looking up the flower on the internet. Take pictures of your favorite flowers and store them in the Souvenir Savor or tape them to the Aloha Memories pages at the end of this book.

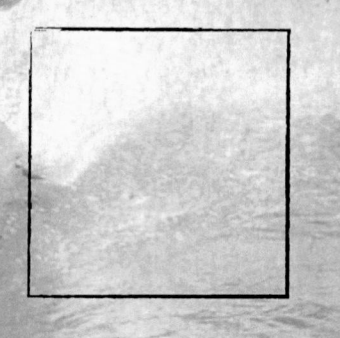

	Flower #1	Flower #2
Red	☐ _____	☐ _____
Yellow	☐ _____	☐ _____
Green	☐ _____	☐ _____
Pink	☐ _____	☐ _____
White	☐ _____	☐ _____
Purple	☐ _____	☐ _____
Multi	☐ _____	☐ _____
Orange	☐ _____	☐ _____

CHALLENGES

Rainbow Chasers
CHALLENGE!

Hawaii is a tropical paradise. It rains a lot to stay that green! All of the moisture in the air creates many rainbows! Tally all the rainbows you see during your visit using the box to the right. At the end, write down your total. Whenever possible, take a picture of the rainbows you see and store your favorites on the pages at the end of this book or in the Souvenir Saver.

Total: _____

Warning Sign
CHALLENGE!

Throughout the islands, there are all sorts of signs that tell you what is coming, what might be coming and what you should be looking for. Many of these signs are unique to Hawaii. As you learn about Hawaii and the places you travel, keep an eye out for the most interesting signs you can find. Take a picture of your favorites and use the space to the ;eft to design your very own sign.

Exploring Different Terrain CHALLENGE!

Hawaii is famous for more than its world famous beaches! One of the cool things about the Hawaiian Islands is their proximity to many different terrains. In under an hour, you can travel from the beach, to dry/arid volcanoes, to tropical rainforests, mountains and sprawling valleys. During your trip, try to visit each of the following: (1) the beach, (2) the mountains, (3) a volcano, and (4) the rainforest. Write down where you visited on the lines to the right. Then take a picture and keep it in your Souvenir Saver.

1. _____

2. _____

3. _____

4. _____

aloha! hawaii

Tape your favorite picture here.

Tip: You can use a mirror to take a picture of yourself taking pictures!

☆GET IT!

Hawaii is a beautiful state that is waiting for you to take memorable pictures. Keep your camera nearby - you never know what you will see! Try to take pictures of all of the items listed on these two pages. Choose a favorite toy or stuffed animal for the Bonus below.

BONUS!

Try to get a favorite toy or stuffed animal in every picture you take during your trip.

- ☐ You sitting inside your suitcase
- ☐ You by your front door
- ☐ You in the car or airplane
- ☐ A grumpy grown-up
- ☐ Your hands or feet in water
- ☐ You on someone's shoulders

- ☐ Eating food on a stick
- ☐ You wearing a snorkel
- ☐ You and a new friend
- ☐ You jumping on the bed
- ☐ Your craziest outfit
- ☐ You, upside down

- ☐ Your worst vacation day
- ☐ Your Hawaiian name
- ☐ You in a tree
- ☐ Someone sleeping
- ☐ You and a tiny dog
- ☐ You taking a picture

Aloha! Hawaii

- [ ] An ice cream shop
- [ ] A helicopter
- [ ] A Hawaii state flag
- [ ] You floating in water
- [ ] A statue
- [ ] A giant wave
- [ ] A red door
- [ ] A grave marker
- [ ] Snorkel Bob's
- [ ] A tourist t-shirt
- [ ] Any city hall
- [ ] An ABC Store
- [ ] People kissing
- [ ] You hula dancing
- [ ] A police car
- [ ] A tropical garden
- [ ] A purple sign
- [ ] A place of worship
- [ ] A flower necklace

Tape your favorite picture here.

Tip: Make sure you keep all of your other pictures in the Souvenir Saver!

- [ ] You in a grass skirt
- [ ] A person riding a bike
- [ ] Something with stripes
- [ ] You on a Boogie Board
- [ ] Seaweed
- [ ] A cupcake store

- [ ] Bubbles
- [ ] A train
- [ ] A horse
- [ ] A blimp
- [ ] A dragon
- [ ] A fountain

- [ ] A turtle
- [ ] An angel
- [ ] A squirrel
- [ ] A pineapple
- [ ] A billboard
- [ ] A fancy car

ARRIVING IN HAWAII

I felt: _____

I went with: _____

The weather was: _____

Hawaii is totally amazing and the weather is great!

Dear _____ ,

Date _____

POST CARD

PLACE STAMP HERE

THIS SIDE FOR MESSAGE

Place cool stamp here!

Tip: If you didn't stay in a hotel, tape any memento of where you stayed during your time in Hawaii.

Did you call home today?

Tape your hotel key.

PLEASE RETURN THIS KEY TO FRONT OFFICE UPON CHECK OUT

PLEASE RETURN THIS KEY TO FRONT OFFICE UPON CHECK OUT

DO IT! ✋

Draw a picture of a special Hawaiian landmark.

Tip: People arrive in Hawaii everyday by airplane and sometimes by boat.

HB-IPU

Tape a picture of how you got to Hawaii.

ARRIVING IN HAWAII

DO IT!
Draw your idea for a Hawaiian flag.

Tape a picture of a Hawaiian freeway sign.

WRITE IT!
Write and illustrate a poem or short story about a child your age who lives in Hawaii. Store your work in the Souvenir Saver.

☆GET IT!
☐ Hawaii map
☐ Parking receipt

FIND IT!
Try to spot these on the road:
☐ Turtle crossing sign
☐ Airport sign

DO IT!
Write four things you've never seen before.

_____

_____

_____

THE BEACH

Tape a picture
of the beach.

Tip: See how many of the items below
you can capture in one picture.

Beach Name:

FIND IT! at the Beach

Find these items at the beach:

- ☐ Bird
- ☐ Litter
- ☐ Beach ball
- ☐ Surfboard
- ☐ Rock
- ☐ Feather
- ☐ Seaweed
- ☐ Sand crab
- ☐ Shell
- ☐ Fish
- ☐ Lifeguard
- ☐ Catamaran

THE BEACH

Tape a picture
of the beach.

Tip: Lighting for pictures at the beach is
best during sunrise and sunset.

Design a Surfboard

Some of the world's most famous
surfboard designs can be seen in
Hawaii. Create your own design
by coloring and decorating the white
surfboard here.

✋ DO IT! Build a Sand Castle

Build a castle with sand
and containers.
Decorate it with shells.
Take a picture and store
it in the Souvenir Saver.

Dig a moat and a
channel from your
castle to the ocean.
When the tide comes
in, it will fill your moat.

OPEN AIR MARKET

INTERNATIONAL MARKET PLACE

Aloha!

Take a picture of an open air market.

Tip: Take a picture of you buying a souvenir.

Hang Loose!

Hawaiians use the Shaka Sign - which means hang loose - to show their "Aloha Spirit." Color the Shaka sign below.

DO IT! Aloha! What did you say?

Open air markets are rich with Hawaiian culture and history. Many words have several meanings, like Aloha, which can mean hello, goodbye, love, kindness and more! Try to use these Hawaiian phrases while shopping in the market:

- ☐ How are you? = Pehea oe? (pey-HEY-ah OH-ey)
- ☐ Goodbye = Aloha (ah-LO-ha)
- ☐ Thank you = Mahalo (ma-HA-lo)
- ☐ Excuse me = E ia nei (EY EE-ah NAY-ee)

- ☐ No = Aole (AH-oh-lay)
- ☐ Hello = Aloha (ah-LO-ha)
- ☐ Please = Olu olu (OH-loo-OH-loo)
- ☐ Yes = Ae (eye)

FARMERS' MARKET

Tape a picture of a farmers' market.

Tip: Take a picture in front of the strangest food you see.

FIND IT!
Flower Market

Walk through the farmers' market and find these flowers or plants:

- [ ] Rose
- [ ] Iris
- [ ] Hibiscus
- [ ] Bonsai
- [ ] Orchid
- [ ] Lavender

- [ ] Gardenia
- [ ] Lavender
- [ ] Anthurium
- [ ] Carnation
- [ ] Firecracker Plant
- [ ] Bird of Paradise

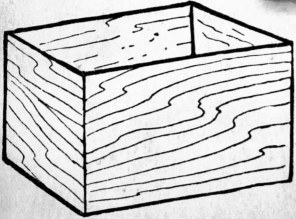

The Farmers' Market sells everything from produce to toys to ice cream. Make a list of all the things you want to buy. Then draw them in the crate.

_____

_____

PLANTATION

Tape a picture from the plantation.

Tip: Get a picture showing you as a farmer on the plantation.

FIND IT!
Plantation Photo Hunt

Find and take a picture of these things!
You'll find some only in the feeding area.

- ☐ Pineapple
- ☐ Fruit Juice
- ☐ Tractor
- ☐ Plantation Animal
- ☐ Farmer
- ☐ Flower
- ☐ Plantation Sign
- ☐ Two Different Varieties of Plantation Food
- ☐ Gift Shop
- ☐ Map of the Plantation
- ☐ Bathroom Item made from Plantation Product

? ANSWER IT! ?

What are four uses for the fruit grown below?

_____

_____

_____

DO IT!

Design a meal using plantation crops.
Be sure you label your creation!

HAWAIIAN SNOW

✋ DO IT!
Design Your Own Hawaiian Snow

Draw your very own Hawaiian Snow concoction in the cup below. To the side, write all of the flavors that you included in your creation. Be sure to give it a name!

Tape a picture of you eating a Hawaiian Snow.

Tip: Take one picture when you start and one when you finish – what a mess!

Name _____

Flavors _____

✋ DO IT! Flavor Mix-up!

Hawaiian Snow comes in many different flavors. Unscramble the following Hawaiian Snow Flavors.

_____ mtWnlaereo

_____ reyCrh

_____ oRto ereB

_____ naiP dolaCa

_____ maniCnon

_____ trbySwerar

_____ totonC danCy

_____ bBblue mGu

Iao Valley

Tape a picture of you in the Iao Valley.

Tip: Take a picture of a very interesting plant or you by the water.

DO IT! Skipping Stone Challenge

There is a good-sized creek in the Iao Valley and skipping stones in the water can be a lot of fun. Find the smoothest, flattest and roundest rocks you can and see how many times you can skip stones on top of the water. Write down the number of "skips" on the lines below.

1st Try ____

2nd Try ____

3rd Try ____

4th Try ____

Most Ever ____

FIND IT! in the Iao Valley

Find these items in the Iao Valley:

- ☐ Bird
- ☐ Fish
- ☐ Frog
- ☐ Litter
- ☐ Feather
- ☐ Log
- ☐ Insect
- ☐ Wild animal
- ☐ Leaf
- ☐ Flash flood sign
- ☐ Colored rock
- ☐ Iao Needle
- ☐ Thatched roof
- ☐ Large boulder
- ☐ Plant growing on a tree.

⚠ WARNING

Flash Flood!

Be alert, water may rise without warning.

Fast moving water in serious...

ALOHA SHIRT

Tape a picture of a you in an aloha shirt.

Tip: Hilo Hatie and the ABC stores have a wide variety of shirts to try on for pics!

Aloha Shirt

Aloha shirts are also called Hawaiian shirts. This style was started in Hawaii and this first Aloha shirt was sold around 1900. Some aloha shirts can cost hundreds of dollars!

Design your own aloha shirt above.

Aloha Shirt Mixup Words

How many words can you make from the letters in "aloha shirt"? Write them on the lines:

_____ _____

_____ _____

_____ _____

FIND IT!

Aloha shirts come in a large variety of colors and designs. Find aloha shirts with these items on them and take pictures trying on your favorites:

☐ Turtles ☐ Hula Girl

☐ Guitars ☐ Surfers

☐ Hawaiian Islands

SNORKELING

Tape a picture of you snorkeling.

Tip: Use an underwater camera or take a picture while on the beach wearing all your gear!

Fishy Friends

The Pacific Ocean is home to many different types of aquatic life. Write down your three favorite animals you saw while snorkeling.

_____

_____

_____

FIND IT!

Look for these while you snorkel. Hint: Snorkel Bob's shops are located all over and they give away free fish ID cards! Put one in the Souvenir Saver.

- ☐ Eel
- ☐ Sea Turtle
- ☐ Octopus
- ☐ Butterfly Fish
- ☐ Needlefish
- ☐ Angel Fish
- ☐ Jellyfish
- ☐ Shark
- ☐ Parrotfish
- ☐ Anenome
- ☐ Yellow Trumpfish
- ☐ Humuhumunukunuku

✎WRITE IT! Silly Fish Story

Jake is a _____ and is more than ___ years old! One day, while _____ near his _____, he met a new
　　　　　　type of fish　　　　　　　　number　　　　　　　　　　　verb　　　　　　　　　　noun
_____ named _____. Most people don't know this, but Herman is quite _____ even
type of animal　　　　　　name 1　　　　　　　　　　　　　　　　　　　　　　　　　　adjective
though he weighs more than 450 pounds. His new friend weighs _____ pounds and she loves to _____. At that
　　　　　　　　　　　　　　　　　　　　　　　　　　ocean　　　　　　　　　　　　　　verb
moment a _____ named _____ jumped into the pond and yelled, "_____". Herman and
　　　　　　fish　　　　　　　　name 2　　　　　　　　　　　　　　　　　exclamation
_____ were startled and both _____. As they did, they heard laughter and realized that this was just a
name 1　　　　　　　　　　　　verb
_____ joke. They looked at each other and _____ and then the decided to _____ happily ever after.
adjective　　　　　　　　　　　　　　　　verb　　　　　　　　　　　　　　　verb

ABC STORE

✋ DO IT!
ABC Souvenir Design

ABC Stores are located all over Hawaii and are full of souvenirs. After searching through the stores to find the items below, create your very own souvenir that you think people would want to buy from an ABC Store in Hawaii. Decide how much you will charge for your Hawaiian souvenir.

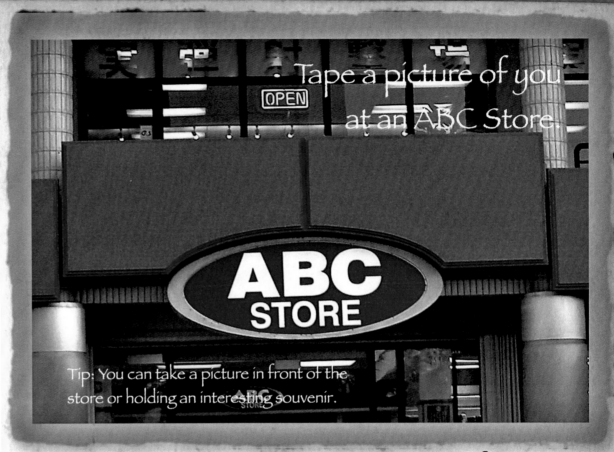

• Tape a picture of you at an ABC Store.

OPEN

ABC STORE

Tip: You can take a picture in front of the store or holding an interesting souvenir.

🔭 FIND IT!
In the ABC Store

Find these items while shopping in the ABC Stores. Take pictures of your favorite souvenirs to save in the Souvenir Saver or to tape in the pages at the back of the book.

- ☐ Macadamia nuts
- ☐ Map of Hawaii
- ☐ Key chain with your Hawaiian name
- ☐ SPAM
- ☐ Kid crying
- ☐ Calendar with Hula dancers
- ☐ Starfish
- ☐ Caramacs chocolates
- ☐ Coasters with a map of the Hawaiian islands
- ☐ Dolphin pen
- ☐ Ring with flowers
- ☐ Playing cards with people in swim suits
- ☐ Bikini drinking glass
- ☐ Aloha shirt
- ☐ Shark tooth necklace

Art Gallery

Tape a picture of an art gallery.

Tip: Take pictures from outside the gallery and try to find an interesting sign!

How Expensive?

Write down the most expensive price you can find for each item as you visit art galleries:

Painting $ _____

Statue $ _____

Photograph $ _____

Cartoon Drawing $ _____

Furniture $ _____

✏ WRITE IT! Shopping Story

On _____, the stores are _____. I searched high and low and
    Hawaiian island   adjective

when I finally spotted a _____, I bought it! It was very _____,
                          piece of art   adjective

_____, and _____. It cost _____ dollars! I think it will look
 adjective   adjective   number

_____ in my room. I cannot wait to show _____ and _____.
 adjective   friend's name   friend's name

I know they'll look at it and _____. Next time, I'll buy a _____!
                               verb   piece of art

✋ DO IT! Window Shop

Browse several art galleries. Keep a list of everything you would buy, how much it cost, and put the list in the Souvenir Saver.

Hawaiian cuisine

? ANSWER IT! ?

Hawaiian cuisine is an interesting combination of many different types of cuisines, including American, Japanese, South Pacific and others. Many foods are similar to those you probably eat every day and some are likely very different. Answer the following questions about things you notice about Hawaiian cuisine.

List 5 menu items that you have never seen before:

_____

_____

_____

_____

_____

The grossest menu item I found was:

_____

The most interesting menu item was:

_____

The item I wanted to try most was:

_____

Something new I tried was:

_____

Tape a picture of the most bizarre Hawaiian cuisine or menu you can find.

Tip: Sometimes our most familiar restaurants - like McDonald's or other chains - make it easiest to spot the biggest differences!

✋ DO IT!

Menu Creation

Make your own menu using the grossest, most interesting and tasty foods you found while traveling in Hawaii. Use the space on the left to create your menu.

MUSEUM

Tape a picture
of a museum that you visited.

Tip: Most museums install interesting art
or landscaping near their entrances.

✋ DO IT! Artwork
Use the blank space below to draw your own masterpiece!

✏ WRITE IT!
Write a story about
your favorite exhibit.
Keep the story in the
Souvenir Saver.

Tape Your
Entrance Ticket

Tip: If you do not have a
ticket, collect a brochure
or other memento.

☆ GET IT!
Put these items in
the Souvenir Saver:

☐ Postcard

☐ Museum guide/map

☐ Museum brochure

Luau

✋ DO IT! Dancers

Luaus feature many different kinds of dancers. While watching the performers, count the number of hula dancers and the number of fire dancers. Write down the total for each and circle your favorite.

Hula Dancers

Total:_____

Fire Dancers

Total:_____

Tape a picture of the luau

Tip: You can take a picture with the dancers or even of the pig!

✏ WRITE IT!

Imagine you are an explorer. You have sailed your ship to the middle of the Pacific Ocean and stumbled across dozens of Hawaiians hosting a luau. What would happen? Write a story about your first experience of a luau, the crazy things you saw (and did!), the food and what happened after the celebration ended. Keep your story in the Souvenir Saver.

✋ DO IT! at the Luau

Luaus are filled with interesting customs, people and food! Take a picture of each of the following and try to get yourself in as many of the pictures as possible.

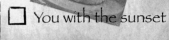

- ☐ Hula dancer
- ☐ You wearing a lei
- ☐ Your holding a tropical drink
- ☐ You doing the hula
- ☐ Fire dancer
- ☐ You eating poi
- ☐ You with a Tiki statue
- ☐ Pig being cooked
- ☐ You with the sunset

MAUI OCEAN CENTER

MAUI OCEAN CENTER

Tape a picture of the front of the ocean center or your favorite exhibit.

Tip: Make a "fishy face" when you take your Maui Ocean Center photo!

✋ DO IT! Biologist

Before there were cameras, marine biologists who found strange sea creatures drew pictures and wrote descriptions to record their discoveries. Draw a picture below of a strange sea creature you find at the center. Put a written description of the animal in the Souvenir Saver.

Sea Star Challenge

Read the paragraph and and identify the parts of the Sea Star. Then color it in!

Sea stars come in many colors, sizes and textures. Most sea stars, also known as starfish, have five <u>rays</u> or arms that make the shape of a star. Sea Stars can have up to 50 or more rays. Each of their rays has little <u>tubed feet</u> along the middle and at the very end of the ray is an <u>eye spot</u>. In the middle of the Sea Star is its <u>mouth</u>.

🔍 FIND IT!

Find and take a picture of these things!

- ☐ Sea star
- ☐ Shark
- ☐ Jellyfish
- ☐ Seahorse
- ☐ Seaweed
- ☐ Anemone
- ☐ Barnacle
- ☐ Seagull

☆ GET IT!

Collect these items during your visit!

- ☐ Brochure
- ☐ Receipt
- ☐ Postcard
- ☐ Ticket

Lahaina

👓 FIND IT!

There are many interesting sites throughout Lahaina. Did you see each of these?

- ☐ Old Lahaina Courthouse
- ☐ Lahaina Public Library
- ☐ The Old Fort / Fort Ruins
- ☐ The Canal
- ☐ Front Street Sign
- ☑ Banyan Tree
- ☐ Wo Hing Museum
- ☐ Baldwin Home Museum
- ☐ A Statue

Take a picture of Lahaina

Tip: Take a picture of you and your family in front of your favorite historic building, tree or statue.

✏ WRITE IT!
Banyan Tree Explorer

When I visited Lahaina's famous Banyan Tree, I saw that it had a _____! The trees at home only have _____. The branches were _____. The leaves were even _____. I think it would be fun to have this tree in my backyard because _____.

✋ DO IT!

Draw a picture of your favorite historic site from Old Lahaina!

Tape a picture of Haleakala.

HALEAKALĀ
NATIONAL PARK

Tip: There are many interesting pictures you can take as you tour the park.

ELEVATION 10,023 FEET (3055 METERS)

☆ DO IT!

There are many things to see and do at Haleakala National Park. Complete the list below during your visit.

Haleakalā National Park
Do Not Feed Nēnē
Keep Them Wild

- [ ] Picture of a silver bush
- [ ] Picture of a Haleakala sign
- [ ] Picture of a NeNe
- [ ] Picture of a NeNe Xing sign
- [ ] Get a Jr. Ranger Guide book
- [ ] Picture of you under the elevation sign

Nēnē Crossing

Tape Your Entrance Ticket

HALEAKALA
NATIONAL PARK
HALEAKALA NP
NON TRANSFERABLE

Auto Pass $10.00

DUE $10.00
CASH $10.00

Keep Your Receipt
VALID THROUGH
8/03/12

☆ GET IT!

At the Visitor Center, inquire about the Junior Ranger Badge. Once you earn yours, tape it here or put it in the Souvenir Saver!

BONUS!

Haleakala, like many parks, offers visitors a free stamp at the Visitor Center. All you have to do is ask! Use the blank space to the right for your stamp.

APR 2 6 2011

ROaD TO HaNa

Historic Highway CHALLENGE! 360

Route 36 and Route 360 make up the majority of the scenic Hana Highway. It stretches more than 50 miles and includes 620 curves and 59 bridges. Tally how many times you curved right and how many times you curved left. Also count how many bridges were only one lane!

Curve Right   Curve Left   One Lane Bridge

_____   _____   _____

☆GET IT!

Put these items from the Road to Hana in the Souvenir Saver:

- ☐ Brochure
- ☐ Leaf
- ☐ Picture in front of a waterfall sign
- ☐ Picture on a bridge

Tape your favorite picture along the Road to Hana.

Tip: The waterfalls make excellent pictures.

FIND IT!

There are countless waterfalls along the Road to Hana, including more than seven major falls. During your drive, see how many signs you can spot and check the box under "Signs". Also, keep track of each of the waterfalls you see by checking the box under "Falls". As a bonus, write the mile marker number nearest the falls!

	Sign	Falls	Nearest Mile Marker
Twin Falls	☐	☐	_____
Waikamoi Stream	☐	☐	_____
Lower Puohokamoa Falls	☐	☐	_____
Ha'ipua'ena Falls	☐	☐	_____
Punalau Falls	☐	☐	_____
Lower Waikani Falls	☐	☐	_____
Wailue Iki Falls	☐	☐	_____

5 M.P.H.

ONE LANE BRIDGE

special ohana meal

Tape a picture from the restaurant.

Tip: Some people like to take a picture of their menu, too!

FIND IT!
Special Diets

Hawaiians follow lots of diets. Find one menu item for each of the following diets:

- ☐ Vegan/Vegetarian
- ☐ Gluten-Free
- ☐ Lactose-Free
- ☐ Low Carb
- ☐ Organic

? ANSWER IT! ?

Our server's name was: _____

The meal I ate was: _____

It tasted: _____

It cost: _____

☆ GET IT!

Collect your receipt, a kid's menu, a coaster, and a napkin. Put them in the Souvenir Saver.

special oHana meal

DO IT! Food Art

Draw a picture of a crazy pizza you would order and then decorate it!

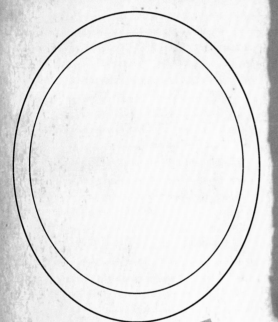

Tape a picture from the restaurant.

Tip: If your server is a lot of fun, try getting a picture with them!.

☆GET IT!

Collect your receipt, a menu, a business card, and a napkin. Put them in the Souvenir Saver or tape one here.

MELLOW MUSHROOM
mellowmushroom.com

?? ANSWER IT! ??

Our server's name was: _____

The meal I ate was: _____

It tasted: _____

It cost: _____

ALOHA MEMORIES

Use these blank pages to tape pictures, maps, receipts, tickets, postcards, and anything else to remember your vacation!

POST CARD

CORRESPONDENCE

ADDRESS

THE OWL STUDIOS

No. 2

7 Federal

North Side

Made by

JACK WEEKS & CO.

PITTSBURGH, PA.

No. 1

105½

Smithfield St.

A PLACE
STAMP
HERE

空郵 PAR AVION
AIR MAIL
CORREO AERE

HONG KONG

22, London Road,
KINGS LYNN,
NORFOLK,
ENGLAND.

ALOHA MEMORIES

POST CARD

CORRESPONDENCE

ADDRESS

PLACE STAMP HERE

No. 1 105½ Smithfield St. Made by THE OWL STUDIOS JACK WEEKS & CO. PITTSBURGH, PA. No. 2 7 Federal St. North Side

PAR AVION
AIR MAIL
CORREO AERE

HONG KONG

22, London Road,

KINGS LYNN,

NORFOLK

ENGLAND.

CORRESPONDENCE ADDRESS

Travelers Series

Metro Area Memory Books

San Diego, CA

Orange County, CA

Los Angeles, CA

Santa Barbara, CA

Monterey, CA

San Francisco, CA

Sacramento, CA

Portland, OR

Hawaii State

Maui, HI

Oahu, HI

Themed Memory Books

California Baseball Stadiums

California Missions

Special Destination Memory Books

Disneyland Resort:

  Disneyland

  Disney California Adventure

  Disneyland and California

  Adventure Combo

Walt Disney World Resort:

  Magic Kingdom

  Epcot

  Disney's Hollywood Studios

  Disney's Animal Kingdom

Universal Orlando Resort:

  Universal Studios Florida &

  Islands of Adventure Combo

Guide Books

Tokyo Disneyland Resort

Upcoming Titles from Travelers Series

Memory Books:

  Las Vegas, NV

  Phoenix, AZ

  Denver, CO

  Seattle, WA

  Austin, TX

  Nashville, TN

Memory Books (Holiday Series):

  Holiday Memories (includes all holidays)

  Christmas

  Thanksgiving

  Summer Vacation

  Winter Holiday

www.TravelersSeries.com

Made in the USA
San Bernardino, CA
14 April 2015